TINA NORDSTRÖM'S RECIPES FOR YOUNG COOKS

Tina's

RECIPE'S FOR

YOUNG
COOKS

• KID-FRIENDLY TIPS AND
TRICKS TO COOK
LIKE A MASTER CHEF •

TINA
NORDSTRÖM

PHOTOGRAPHY: JENNY GRIMSGÅRD

TRANSLATION: GUN PENHOAT

SKYHORSE PUBLISHING

CONTENTS

7 HI!

9 KITCHEN BASICS 101

21 GOOD MORNING!

35 COOKING WEEKDAY MEALS

51 DAZZLE THE GROWNUPS

67 HANGING OUT WITH FRIENDS

83 SWEETS

96 INDEX

HI!

Cooking is awesome, isn't it? There's nothing better than hanging out in the kitchen and just chopping, mixing, stirring, cooking, and tasting. Often it's not as hard as it looks; with great recipes and some solid tips, you can rustle up a lot more than you ever imagined.

For this book, I've selected simple recipes, as well as some that are a bit more challenging. You can prepare a lot of these recipes by yourself, but there are a few dishes included here for which you'll need some assistance from an adult. Then, invite your family and friends over for breakfast, dinner, or a party! They'll leave feeling happy and full—I promise.

If something doesn't turn out quite as expected, well, it's not the end of the world. All chefs have off-moments like that. And who knows, next time you try that same dish it could turn out better than expected! Practice makes perfect, but don't forget—cooking should be fun.

Here's my best tip for you: Taste the food as you go along, stirring and mixing whatever's in the pots and pans. You might find that you need to add an extra pinch of salt or some other spice, which could make all the difference.

Get that apron on and let's get to work!

Tina

KITCHEN BASICS 101

I don't believe cooking should be serious business. However, there are a few basic tips that can make time spent in the kitchen way more fun, and easier, too. Here I've laid out what you need to know before you begin prepping food—what tools you'll need to have on hand, how to cook pasta, and other important information. It's not a bad idea at all to go over some Kitchen Basics 101!

1 Lesson

BEFORE YOU BEGIN

Carefully read through the entire recipe, and check that you have all the ingredients you need.

Think through each step so you know what you have to do. Perhaps you need to get something out of the freezer to let it defrost.

Pull out all the ingredients, and then follow the steps of the recipe from start to finish.

CLEAN AND ORDERLY

Wash your hands. I recommend that you put on an apron, too.

Use separate cutting boards for vegetables, meat, chicken, and fish. Or, make sure to wash the cutting board thoroughly if you're only using one board for the whole recipe.

Try to wash, dry, and put away the pots and utensils when you're done with them as you go along so you don't come face to face with a sink full of dirty dishes when you're done cooking.

FRESHLY GROUND PEPPER

Pepper is always best when it's freshly ground; it has far more flavor. Always grind whole peppercorns using a pepper mill, instead of using bottled pre-ground pepper. Keep a mill for black pepper, and a separate one for white pepper.

MEASURING AND WEIGHING

The ingredients list will tell you how much of each item you will need for a recipe. If you must know how much something weighs, check the packaging, or use a kitchen scale. The wrapper on the butter has equally spaced lines that will guide you in using the correct amount; each line is equal to 1¾ oz (50 g).

Flour, sugar, milk, and many other ingredients are measured with sets of measuring cups and spoons. Each measuring cup set typically includes 1 cup, ½ cup (1 dl), and ¼ cup (½ dl); spoon sets typically come with 1 tablespoon (1 tbsp) and 1 teaspoon (1 tsp). If a recipe calls for ½ cup (1 dl) of flour, you will scoop some flour using the ½ cup (1 dl), and slide a finger across the top of the cup to remove any excess flour to make exactly ½ cup (1 dl) of flour.

It's especially important to pay close attention to the recipe's amounts when you bake. If the directions say "3 large eggs" choose a carton with large eggs. If you use eggs that are too small, the cake might not turn out as intended.

VOLUME MEASUREMENTS
4¼ cups (1 = liter)
½ cup (1 dl = deciliter)
Tbsp (msk) = tablespoon
Tsp (tsk) = teaspoon
⅕ tsp (1 krm)

4¼ cups (1 liter = 10 dl) 1 tbsp = 3 tsp

WEIGHT MEASUREMENTS
2¼ lbs (1 kg)
0.03 oz (1 g)

2¼ lbs (1 kg = 1,000 g)

2%

WHEN COOKING WITH MILK

If the recipe calls for milk, don't use fat-free or low-fat milk, but milk with higher fat content, like 2% or whole.

2

Lesson

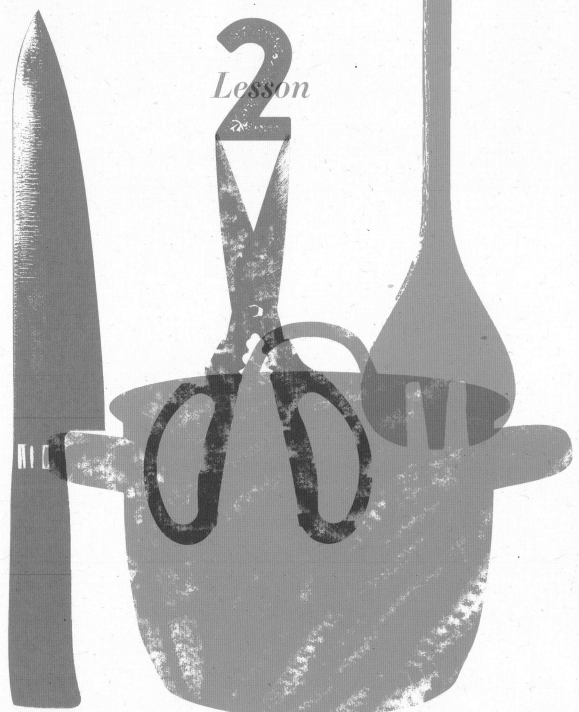

MUST-HAVE KITCHEN UTENSILS

ROLLING PIN. An absolute necessity for rolling out bread or pasta dough.

BOWLS. Needed for when you mix and whip different ingredients together. It's good to have several bowls in a variety of sizes.

STRAINER/COLANDER. Used to strain off pasta water and rinse vegetables or lettuce.

POT HOLDER/OVEN GLOVE. To avoid burning yourself when you remove hot dishes and baking sheets from the oven.

KITCHEN SCALES. Good to have if you need to weigh ingredients.

SAUCEPANS. For stovetop cooking. You might need different sizes.

KNIVES. A serrated bread knife and a few really sharp knives are good to have on hand. Always be extremely careful when handling sharp knives!

A SET OF PLASTIC MEASURING CUPS AND SPOONS. Often a small set with ½ cup (1 dl), ¼ cup (½ dl), 1 tbsp (1 msk), and 1 tsp (1 tsk).

POTATO RICER. You might not use it very often, but boiled riced potatoes are so good that you'll want a ricer!

POTATO PEELER. For peeling potatoes, of course, but it's also handy for peeling other root vegetables and fruits.

BOX GRATER. The best grater is one that you can stand upright on your cutting board. It has several sides with different sized grating surfaces, ranging from coarse to fine.

SALAD SPINNER. Great for drying lettuce leaves after you've washed them.

A PAIR OF KITCHEN SHEARS. Good for cutting chunks of bacon or slices of pizza, for example.

SIEVE. You can rinse jasmine or basmati rice in a fine mesh sieve. You can also mash berries or potatoes into a purée by passing them through a sieve.

SPATULAS. They are typically made of rubber or silicone. Use them for scraping food out of bowls, such as whipped cream or cake batter.

SOUP LADLE. For serving soup.

IMMERSION BLENDER/FOOD PROCESSOR. Perfect for blending smoothies or making soup.

FRYING PAN/SKILLET. It can be cast iron, or have a nonstick coating to prevent fried foods from sticking.

GRILL TONGS. You can use these for turning pieces of meat in a frying pan.

FRYING SPATULA. You'll need one for flipping pancakes or meat in the frying pan.

MEAT THERMOMETER. This is used to take the internal temperature of meat and chicken to ensure they're properly cooked.

TIMER. Keeps time when something is cooking in the oven or on the stove.

WOODEN SPOON, LADLE, OR FORK. Good to have on hand for mixing in a bowl.

CORER. For when you need to core a whole apple.

WHISK/ELECTRIC MIXER. Useful for whipping cream and whisking a sauce or a cake batter. An electric mixer gets the job done much quicker than whisking by hand.

OTHER USEFUL KITCHEN TOOLS:
ALUMINUM FOIL
PARCHMENT PAPER
PASTRY BRUSH
PLASTIC WRAP

Lesson 3

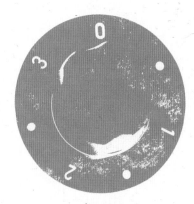

THE STOVETOP

Stoves come in many shapes and sizes. Some have burners enclosed in flat glass surfaces; others have cast iron burners (these are more common in older stoves). Many of today's ranges are fitted with induction surfaces, which heat up and cool off super-fast. And, of course, you have gas ranges with which you cook over a gas flame.

Some stoves have knobs that you turn to increase or reduce the heat, while others have control pads that work with a light tap of a finger. On some stoves the heat can be changed in increments of twelve (on some there are even half-increments), while others only go up or down by four or six. Get to know how your own stove works, and don't forget to turn it off once you're done cooking!

MICROWAVE OVEN

This is a good oven for heating up and defrosting food. You can also melt chocolate and cook vegetables in it.

OVEN

Ovens often have several functions that you can manipulate by using their different knobs or touch pads. You have to select the oven function and the temperature when you want to cook something in the oven. It is becoming more common to find recipes that call for a convection oven, or the oven's convection setting. When you use the convection function, you'll need to reduce the oven's temperature by 20–30 degrees compared to the oven's conventional setting. If you don't make this adjustment, the oven will end up running too hot.

BLENDER AND FOOD PROCESSOR

With a standard or immersion blender, you can whip up smoothies and puréed soups, such as the smoothie on p. 23, and the cauliflower soup on p. 37.

If you're using an immersion blender, it's important that you keep the stick part below the surface of whatever you're mixing, or you'll end up splattering smoothie or soup all over the kitchen! Be careful not to cut yourself on the sharp, rotating knife blades.

In a food processor you can prepare a piecrust, for instance, or chop nuts or almonds. You'll be using the knife attachment for that. You can also slice or grate potatoes and carrots; it's practical to use if you need to process large quantities.

DEEP FRYER

It's best and safest to use a deep fryer to cook your own fries. Thanks to the fryer's built-in thermostat, the oil can never get too hot and start a fire, but it's always best to have an adult around when you want to deep-fry something!

4

Lesson

RINSE AND PEEL

It's very important to rinse fruit, vegetables, and root vegetables—even if it's organic produce. Bagged lettuce leaves usually don't require rinsing, but the whole heads of lettuce often have grit between the leaves. Rinse the leaves under cold running water and dry them in a salad spinner or shake them thoroughly.

You can also find a lot of sand hidden in leeks, so slice them in half lengthwise and then rinse thoroughly between the leaves under running water.

Conventionally grown lemons, limes, and oranges are sprayed with pesticides, so it's critical that you wash them first in lukewarm water and scrub them with a brush if you intend to use the fruit's peel. However, it's best to buy organic citrus fruit.

Many fruits and root vegetables have to be peeled. A potato peeler is useful for a lot of them, but for the really thick peels you'll need to use a knife. New potatoes only need to be scrubbed clean with a brush or with the rough side of a dish sponge.

CUT AND CHOP

Many chefs would probably agree that a sharp knife is the most important tool in the kitchen. It's pretty much impossible to cut meat and onions with a dull knife; you also run a higher risk of getting hurt if your knife is blunt rather than sharp.

When a recipe tells you to chop something really fine, you will need to use a large, sharp knife; what we call a chef's knife.

THIS IS HOW YOU CHOP AN ONION. With a knife, cut the onion into two halves, from top to bottom. Peel the onion. Place one of the onion halves, cut side down, and cut thin slices toward the bottom, but not all the way through. Keeping the onion pieces together, now cut them in the other direction, straight across the slices, so you end up with finely diced onion. Repeat this with the other onion half. Watch out so you don't cut your fingertips!

GRATE AND PRESS

There's a big difference between something that is coarsely grated and something that is finely grated, so follow each recipe's instructions closely. Parmesan cheese is often grated on the box grater's fine side, while carrots are grated on the coarse side.

You can squeeze a lime directly over food, but lemons often contain seeds so they need to be squeezed with a citrus press. Or, you can squeeze a lemon directly into the palm of your hand so the seeds stay in your hand while the juice drips from between your fingers.

USING GARLIC. Forget the garlic press; crush a clove of garlic and chop it fine. Place an unpeeled clove of garlic on a chopping board. Take a large knife and set its blade flat on top of the clove, then smash it down with your hand. This will crush the clove and loosen the peel so it can be easily removed. Finely chop the clove or leave it whole to add flavor when you cook meat and vegetables. Best of all, you don't have to clean the garlic press!

CRACKING EGGS

To separate the yolk from the egg white, tap the egg's shell against the edge of a bowl so the shell cracks. Hold the egg over the bowl and carefully separate the two halves without spilling the contents of the egg or breaking the yolk. Shift the egg yolk back and forth between the two shells while letting the egg white fall into the bowl. Do this carefully so the yolk doesn't break against the sharp edges of the shell.

If you wish to make meringue with egg whites, it's critical that there be absolutely no yolk at all in the whites, because if there is, it will be impossible to whip the whites up hard enough for meringue.

Lesson 5

BOIL AND SIMMER

When something needs to boil, turn the burner to a high heat until the water bubbles vigorously and large bubbles break the surface. When something needs to simmer, turn the heat down low until you only see tiny bubbles reaching the water's surface.

If you pour cold water into a saucepan and watch it come to a boil, you'll see it first come to a simmer with small, little bubbles. When the water boils at 212°F (100°C) — the bubbles become bigger.

HOW TO BOIL POTATOES. Peel the potatoes and put them in a saucepan or leave the peel on and simply brush them clean. (You will have to peel them if you are making mashed potatoes). Pour cold water into the saucepan until it just covers the top of the potatoes. Add about ½ tsp of salt to the water, and place a lid on the saucepan.

Place the saucepan on a burner set to the highest heat. Once the water is boiling, turn the heat down and cook the potatoes until they are soft. Check for doneness by piercing one of the potatoes with a toothpick or fork. Pour the water from the saucepan into the sink by holding the lid up to the saucepan so the water drains through a narrow gap between the saucepan and lid. Be careful not to burn yourself on the hot water!

HOW TO COOK RICE. Pour water and some salt into a saucepan; how much of each depends on how many people you're feeding. The directions on the packet of rice will tell you how much you need. Bring the water to a boil and add the rice. Reduce the heat, stir, and place a lid on the saucepan. Let the rice absorb all the water while simmering slowly; this will take about 20 minutes.

You'll need to rinse off some of the natural starch from jasmine and basmati rice before cooking it, or else it will turn into mush. Place the right amount of rice into a sieve and rinse it thoroughly with cold running water. Jasmine and basmati rice go really well with Indian and Asian dishes.

HOW TO COOK PASTA. Pour 2 to 3 quarts (2 to 3 liters) of cold water or water you have boiled in a kettle in a large saucepan. Place a lid on the saucepan and set the burner on its highest heat. Let the water come to a complete boil and then add ½ tbsp salt per quart of water. Add the pasta to the boiling water and let it cook, uncovered, as long as suggested on the package.

Drain the water off by transferring the pasta to a colander placed over another saucepan or in the kitchen sink. Or, using a kitchen towel, hold down the lid on the saucepan while leaving a narrow gap between lid and pan for the water to drain through into the sink. Be very careful not to burn yourself on the scalding water! Leave the pasta in the saucepan.

FRY, SIZZLE, AND BROWN

You can fry food in different ways. If you are frying something such as onions over a low temperature, they should not take on any color. However, if the recipe says to brown something, then what you're frying should turn brown.

If you are frying over medium heat, the heat needs to be set to half of the stove's setting, or to medium. When you place a pat of butter in a hot skillet, the butter will start to sputter and bubble; only when it has settled down is it time to add the item(s) you are going to fry.

Never crowd the skillet with too many chunks of meat. If you do, the pan will stay too cool to fry anything properly, and the meat will end up steaming instead of frying. Always fry in batches, and place the cooked food to the side as you finish up frying the remaining bits.

MEAT NEEDS TO REST. It is important to let a large piece of meat rest for a while after you have fried it. If you cut into it right away, all the meat's delicious juices will run onto the cutting board instead of staying in the meat and keeping it juicy.

GOOD MORNING!

It's the weekend—finally!—after a never-ending week at school. It's time to get up and out of bed to make a scrumptious breakfast for the whole family! Make crêpes, mix smoothies, or bake scones.

PEACH MELBA SMOOTHIE

Raspberries and peaches are totally meant for each other, so this smoothie is heavenly.
Just mix and pour!

SERVES 4

1 banana
1 (15 oz or 425 g) can of peaches in syrup
1¾ cup (4 dl) frozen raspberries
1¾ cup (4 dl) vanilla yogurt

DIRECTIONS:

1. Peel the banana and cut it into chunks. Put the chunks in a tall container or in a pitcher.

2. Drain the syrup from the peaches, and add the peaches to the container along with the raspberries and the vanilla yogurt.

3. Mix everything in the container with an immersion blender, or transfer to a blender and mix until smooth.

4. Pour into glasses and enjoy.

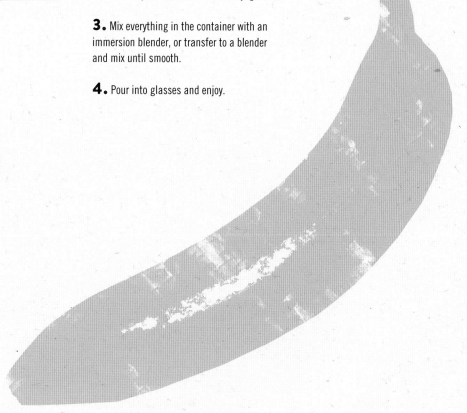

CRÊPES
with chocolate whipped cream and fresh berries

Making crêpes is a blast. They can be a bit tricky to flip sometimes, but with a large spatula and some practice they'll turn out just great.

SERVES 4

CRÊPES:

3 tbsp butter + extra for frying

3 large eggs

1¼ cups (2½ dl) all-purpose flour

½ tsp salt

2½ cups (6 dl) whole milk

CHOCOLATE WHIPPED CREAM:

1¼ cups (3 dl) whipping cream

3 tbsp cocoa

½ tsp vanilla sugar

1 tbsp granular sugar

1¾ oz (50 g) dark chocolate

ACCOMPANIMENT:

Fresh berries, such as raspberries and blueberries

DIRECTIONS:

Start by making the crêpes:

1. Melt 3 tbsp of butter in a saucepan over medium heat. Then set it aside to cool a little.

2. Break the eggs into a bowl, then add the flour, salt, and ¾ cup (2 dl) of milk. Whisk it to make a smooth batter. Add in the melted butter and the rest of the milk and whisk a bit more until there are no lumps.

3. Put extra butter for frying in a skillet (or a crêpe pan) and heat it over medium heat.

4. Pour approximately ⅓ cup (¾ dl) of batter into the frying pan when the butter has melted and begun to sizzle. Keep rotating the pan so the batter spreads over the entire bottom of the pan. Cook until the crêpe starts to solidify on top.

5. Loosen the crêpe from the edge and base of the pan with a spatula, and flip the crêpe over on its other side. Cook for another minute or so and then set the finished crêpe on a plate.

6. Place another pat of butter in the pan. Pour batter into the pan to cook the next crêpe, repeating the previous steps until all the batter is used up.

Make the chocolate whipped cream:

7. Mix whipping cream and cocoa in a bowl and let it sit for a bit. Mix in the vanilla sugar and sugar, then whip the cream until it's fluffy. Put the cream in a bowl and use a box grater's fine side to grate some dark chocolate on top.

Time to eat:

8. Dig in and enjoy the crêpes with a side of chocolate whipped cream and fresh berries.

THE FIRST ATTEMPT IS RARELY PERFECT

The first crêpe is often a bit misshapen. Don't fret, the next one will be better.

FRENCH TOAST

Dip a slice of French bread in some crêpe batter, and fry it in some butter in a skillet. To finish, dip the fried bread in sugar and ground cinnamon.

CARDAMOM SCONES
with Parmesan cheese and Parma ham

Scones are so easy to make. These are slightly reminiscent of coffee buns because of the cardamom, but if you don't like the taste of it you can leave it out.

MAKES 24 SCONES

3½ oz (100 g) butter, softened

3½ cups (8 dl) all-purpose flour

½ cup (1 dl) rolled oats

5 tsp baking powder

1 tsp salt

1¾ cup (4 dl) whole milk or plain yogurt

1 tbsp granular sugar

½–1 tsp ground cardamom

ACCOMPANIMENT:

Philadelphia-style cream cheese

Slices of Parmesan cheese

Slices of Parma ham, smoked ham, or turkey

DIRECTIONS:

1. To soften butter, remove it from the refrigerator about half an hour before you start baking.

2. Preheat the oven to 435°F (225°C).

3. Place all the ingredients except the accompaniments in a bowl. Mix everything together with a wooden fork or large spoon to make dough. The dough will be sticky, but don't add any extra flour because this will make the scones dry.

4. Dust the kitchen countertop with a little flour. Take the dough out of the bowl and put it onto the floured surface. Cut the dough into 6 approximately equal pieces with a dough scraper or a knife.

5. Line a baking sheet with some parchment paper and place the pieces of dough onto the sheet. Dust your hands with flour, and flatten the pieces of dough with your palms. Score a cross in each piece of dough with a sharp knife, but don't cut straight through the dough; the 4 sections should still be attached together.

6. Place the sheet on the middle rack of the oven and bake the scones for about 15 minutes. Check on them now and then, and remove them from the oven when they are golden brown.

7. Let the scones cool slightly on the baking sheet.

Time to eat:

8. Break the scones into 4 pieces and slice through them to make a top and a bottom piece. Slather with cream cheese, add slices of Parmesan cheese and ham. They go great with a cup of tea or a glass of milk.

HAVE LEFTOVER SCONES?

Break the scones into small chunks and toast them on a baking sheet in a 390°F (200°C) oven for about 10 minutes. They're tasty sprinkled over a salad.

GOOD MORNING!

GRANOLA
with nuts and chocolate

This is *sooo* good! You can't buy this kind of granola or muesli at the store. The Swedish word "Hemmagjord" means homemade, and it the best.

MAKES ABOUT 4¼ CUPS (1 LITER/10 DL)

3½ fl oz (1 dl) hazelnuts
1¼ cups (3 dl) rolled oats
1¼ cup (3 dl) Rice Krispies cereal
¾ cup (2 dl) coconut flakes or grated coconut
½ cup (1 dl) pumpkin seeds
½ cup (1 dl) unsalted peanuts
½ cup (1 dl) water
1¾ oz (50 gr) coconut oil
½ cup (1 dl) honey
¼ cup (½ dl) cocoa powder
1 tbsp vanilla sugar

ACCOMPANIMENT:

Honey
Berries, sliced apple, or other fruit

DIRECTIONS:

1. Preheat the oven to 350°F (175°C).

2. Chop the hazelnuts coarsely with a knife.

3. Mix the hazelnuts, rolled oats, Rice Krispies, coconut flakes, pumpkin seeds, and peanuts together in a bowl.

4. Pour water, coconut oil, honey, cocoa powder and vanilla sugar into a saucepan and bring to a boil on the stove. Pour this liquid over the nut and grain mixture in the bowl. Stir thoroughly with a wooden fork.

5. Line a baking sheet with some parchment paper, pour the nut mixture onto it, and spread it out evenly over the paper.

6. Place the baking sheet on the middle rack of the oven and roast the granola for 25 to 30 minutes. The liquid will be absorbed, and the granola will clump up a bit. Keep a close watch on things so it doesn't burn!

7. Remove the baking sheet from the oven and let the granola cool completely. Store the granola in a glass jar with a lid.

Time to eat:

8. Sprinkle some granola over yogurt or cultured milk. By all means, drizzle with some honey and serve with fruit or berries.

FRUIT SALAD
with pineapple, passion fruit, and mint

You don't need lots of fruit to make a salad. Here we have only two types—and it's all we need.
Try it!

SERVES 4

1 fresh pineapple
3 passion fruits
1 bunch mint

ACCOMPANIMENT:

Whipped cream or ice cream

DIRECTIONS:

1. Peel the pineapple and dice it as large as you like. Place the pineapple chunks in a bowl or on a platter.

2. Cut the passion fruits in half. Hold the halves above the bowl or platter and spoon out the juice and fruit. Mix the two fruits.

3. Chop the mint leaves and sprinkle them over the fruit.

Time to eat:

4. Enjoy the salad with a dollop of whipped cream or ice cream.

HOW CAN YOU TELL IF THE PINEAPPLE IS RIPE?

Tug on some of the innermost leaves on the pineapple, and if they loosen easily the fruit is ready to eat.

HOW TO PEEL A PINEAPPLE

With a sharp knife, cut off the crown of leaves at the top of the pineapple, and cut off the bottom, too. Stand the pineapple on a cutting board and cut off the peel all around the fruit. Then cut it into 4 pieces lengthwise and remove the hard middle section, as this bit isn't all that nice to eat.

COOKING WEEKDAY MEALS

Time is often in short supply during the week, so imagine your family's delight if you invited them to sit down to a meal of ragu Bolognese or cauliflower soup with a zippy touch of chili and lime, all prepared by you. Who knows, you might even notice a bump in your weekly allowance!

CAULIFLOWER SOUP
with chili and lime

You might think you don't like cauliflower (why wouldn't you?), but believe me, this mellow soup tastes wonderful.

SERVES 4

1 medium-sized cauliflower
½ yellow onion
2 cloves garlic
½ red chili pepper
Oil, for frying
1¾–2 cups (4–5 dl) water
1¾ cups (4 dl) whole milk
¾ cup (2 dl) crème fraîche
1 lime
Salt and freshly ground white pepper

ACCOMPANIMENT:

4 tsp sesame seeds
1–1½ tbsp olive oil
Sea salt flakes

DIRECTIONS:

1. Remove the green leaves from the cauliflower, and cut out the hard middle core. Rinse the cauliflower and cut it into chunks.

2. Peel and chop the onion and garlic. Slice the chili pepper in half, remove its seeds, and then chop it finely.

3. Heat some oil in a large saucepan over medium heat. Add in the cauliflower, onion, garlic, and chopped chili; fry it all up in the oil for a few minutes while stirring often.

4. Add the water and milk, and bring it to a boil. Reduce the heat, cover the pan with a lid, and let the soup simmer until the cauliflower has softened; this will take about 15 minutes.

5. Add in the crème fraîche in dollops, and purée the soup directly in the saucepan with an immersion blender. The soup should be smooth. Bring it quickly back to a boil again.

6. Cut the lime in half and squeeze the juice right into the soup. Season with salt and pepper to taste. Stir.

7. Roast the sesame seeds in a frying pan over medium heat (you don't have to add butter or oil) until they take on a nice color. Keep a close watch on them, as they burn easily!

Time to eat:

8. Ladle the soup into bowls, drizzle with some olive oil, and sprinkle with sesame seeds and some flaky sea salt.

HOW TO JUICE A LIME

The easiest way to get juice from a lime is to first roll the lime on the kitchen counter while pressing down on it slightly with your hand. Then cut the lime in half and squeeze out the juice.

BE CAREFUL WHEN HANDLING CHILI PEPPERS

Once you've sliced open a chili pepper and removed its seeds, always wash your hands thoroughly. If you don't, it will sting something fierce if you rub your eyes with your unwashed fingers.

SALMON AND PASTA GRATIN
with beet salad

You can prepare this gratin in advance if you like. Cook the pasta the evening before, and spoon it into the dish the next day. Wear a pair of kitchen gloves when you grate the beets if you don't want to end up with red hands.

SERVES 4

PASTA GRATIN:
10½ oz (300 g) penne or farfalle pasta
14 oz (400 g) skinless salmon fillet
1 small bunch broccoli
7 oz (200 g) hard, aged cheese
3 large eggs
¾ cup (2 dl) crème fraîche
1¼ cup (3 dl) whole milk
Salt
Freshly ground black or white pepper

BEET SALAD:
3 medium beets
2 stalks celery
¼ cup (½ dl) walnuts
1 lemon
2 tbsp light corn syrup
Freshly ground black pepper

DIRECTIONS:

Pasta gratin:

1. Preheat the oven to 350°F (175°C).

2. Cook the pasta; check the package for specific cooking times. Drain off the water and leave the pasta in the saucepan.

3. Dice the salmon fillet; the pieces should be about 1¼ to 2¼" (3–4 cm). Cut the broccoli into small florets.

4. Grate the cheese using the grater's fine side.

5. Whisk together the eggs and the crème fraîche in a bowl, and then mix in the milk.

6. Stir in half the grated cheese; season with salt and pepper.

7. Place the pieces of salmon and the broccoli florets with the pasta in the saucepan. Add in the cheese sauce and mix. Now pour it all into an oven-safe dish and sprinkle with the remaining grated cheese. Place the dish on the middle rack of the oven and bake for 20 to 25 minutes.

Prepare the beet salad while the gratin is cooking in the oven:

8. Peel the beets and rinse the stalks of celery. First grate the beets and then the celery stalks on the grater's coarse side. It can be hard work to grate the beets by hand; a food processor can make the work go easier. Layer the grated vegetables onto a serving platter.

9. Chop the walnuts and sprinkle them over the salad. Cut the lemon in half and squeeze the juice from both halves, making sure no seeds end up in the salad. Drizzle with syrup and season with freshly ground black pepper.

Time to eat:

10. Remove the pasta gratin from the oven once it is ready, and enjoy with the beet salad.

HOW TO AVOID DYEING EVERYTHING RED

Grate the beets on top of a sheet of parchment paper; that way you avoid splashing the beets' intensely colored juice all over the kitchen counter or cutting board.

Learn how to cook pasta on p. 19.

SAUSAGE STROGANOFF
with Moroccan rice

This is my very favorite rice. Stroganoff makes me want to dance with happiness!

SERVES 4

SAUSAGE STROGANOFF:

14 oz (400 gr) Falukorv or other sausage

7–10½ oz (3 whole or 200–300 g) spicy pork sausages such as salsiccia

3 small yellow onions

½ lb (250 g) roasted whole bell pepper (½ jar of roasted peppers)

1 tbsp olive oil

1¾ lb (800 g) canned crushed tomatoes

½ cup (1 dl) whipping cream

½ tsp salt

MOROCCAN RICE:

1¼ cup (3 dl) Basmati rice

1 tsp cold-pressed canola oil

1½ tsp salt

1 tsp turmeric

1 tsp cumin

1 tsp ground coriander

⅕ tsp (1 krm) ground cardamom

⅕ tsp (1 krm) ground cloves

2½ cup (6 dl) water

DIRECTIONS:

Start with the Stroganoff:

1. Remove the casing from the sausage. Cut the sausage in half lengthwise, and slice into half-moon-shaped slices.

2. Cut the spicy sausages on the bias in ⅓-inch thick (1 cm) slices.

3. Peel and chop the onions or grate them with a box grater. Pour out the liquid from the jar of roasted peppers and slice them. The uglier the chunks, the tastier the dish!

4. Heat the olive oil in a saucepan. Add the onion and pepper and sauté for a few minutes, stirring occasionally with a spoon or fork. Add in all the sausage and keep frying for a few more minutes.

5. Stir in the crushed tomatoes and the cream. Reduce the heat and let the sauce simmer for about 20 minutes.

Cook the rice while the Stroganoff is simmering:

6. Put the rice in a sieve and rinse it thoroughly with cold water. Place the rice in a saucepan and add the oil, salt, and spices. Heat and stir.

7. Add the water and place a lid on the saucepan. Bring the rice to a boil and then reduce the heat. The rice should simmer (there should be some movement in the pan, but no bubbling) for 20 minutes.

Time to eat:

8. Serve the Sausage Stroganoff with the Moroccan rice.

Learn how to cook rice on p. 19.

MEATLOAF
with Parmesan mashed potatoes and green salad

This is really smart weekday food. Just mix everything together and put it in the oven.
I've added some edge to the mash with some Parmesan and lemon.

SERVES 6

MEATLOAF:

1 yellow onion

3 garlic cloves

1 large egg

⅔ cup (1½ dl) whole milk

2 slices of white bread

2¼ lb (1 kg or 1000 g) ground meat, half beef, half pork

2 tsp salt

Freshly ground black or white pepper

2 packages (5 oz or 140 g each) of bacon

PARMESAN MASHED POTATOES:

1¾ lb (800 g) potatoes

Salt, for cooking water

¾ cup (2 dl) whole milk

1¾ oz (50 g) butter

4¼ oz (120 g) Parmesan cheese or Grana Padano

1 tsp salt

Freshly ground black or white pepper

½ lemon, for seasoning

ACCOMPANIMENT:

1 bag (2½ oz or 70 g) of assorted lettuce leaves

DIRECTIONS:

Start with the meatloaf:

1. Preheat the oven to 350°F (175°C).

2. Peel and finely chop the onion and garlic.

3. Crack the egg into a bowl. Pour in the milk and whisk with a fork until mixed. Remove the crust from the slices of bread and set the bread into the egg/milk mixture. Let the bread soak for about 10 minutes.

4. Mix the ground meat with the chopped onion, garlic, and soaked bread. Season the mix with salt and freshly ground pepper.

5. Place the meat mixture on a rimmed baking sheet or in an ovenproof dish. With clean hands, form a loaf. Arrange the slices of bacon over the top of the loaf and tuck in the ends of the bacon under the loaf to keep everything together.

6. Place the meatloaf on the middle rack of the oven and cook it for about 50 minutes. It is ready to eat when the meat's juice runs clear.

Make the mashed potatoes while the meatloaf is in the oven:

7. Boil the potatoes in a large saucepan with salted water. Pour off the water and place the potatoes, a few at a time, in a potato press, or mash by hand. Mash the potatoes back into the saucepan (but don't place the saucepan back on the burner again). Add in the milk and butter, and whip everything to make a smooth purée.

8. Finely grate the Parmesan with a grater and mix the cheese into the potato purée. Season with salt and freshly ground pepper, and squeeze in as much lemon juice as you like. Don't start out with too much, however; add a little at a time.

Time to eat:

9. Remove the meatloaf from the oven. Slice it into ¾ inch (2 cm) slices; enjoy the meatloaf with the mashed potatoes, the salad, and a glass of milk.

TAKE CARE NOT TO OVERSALT
There is a lot of salt in cheese already, so be careful not to make your mash too salty.

TIP FOR SEASONING WITH LEMONS
You can add grated lemon peel to the mash instead of lemon juice, if you like; the mash will have a more intense lemon flavor.

Learn how to cook potatoes on p. 19.

RAGU BOLOGNESE

Ragu Bolognese is for Italians what the rest of us call "spaghetti with meat sauce."
I add some smoked pork belly to make the sauce extra tasty.

SERVES 4–6

PASTA:

14 oz–1¼ lb (400–500 g) spaghetti

MEAT SAUCE:

1 yellow onion

2 garlic cloves

7 oz (200 g) smoked pork belly

3 tbsp olive oil for frying

1½ lb (700 g) ground beef or mixed pork and beef

2 tbsp tomato purée

1¼ cup (3 dl) water

1¾ lb (800 g) canned crushed tomatoes

1 tsp dried thyme

2 tsp dried Mediterranean oregano

1 tsp dried sage

1 tsp salt

Freshly ground white or black pepper

3–4 tbsp olive oil

ACCOMPANIMENT:

Grated Parmesan

Chopped parsley

DIRECTIONS:

Start with the meat sauce:

1. Peel and finely chop the onion and garlic. Dice the pork.

2. Heat the olive oil in a saucepan or Dutch oven, and fry the onion, garlic, smoked pork, and ground meat. Add in the tomato purée, water, crushed tomatoes, thyme, oregano, and sage, and let everything simmer over low heat for about 45 to 50 minutes, or until the sauce thickens.

3. Season the sauce with salt, freshly ground pepper, and olive oil.

Cook the pasta once the sauce is ready:

4. Cook the pasta (check the package for cooking instructions). Drain off the water through a colander.

Time to eat:

5. Transfer the pasta to a large serving bowl and mix in the sauce; that's the Italian way! Top with grated Parmesan and chopped parsley.

Learn how to cook pasta on p. 19.

ASIAN BEEF STEW
with noodles ·

Grated coconut works better than coconut milk in a stew—that's my humble opinion, anyway.
The flavor is milder and the grated coconut adds a more pleasant texture.
Everybody prefers it that way—except maybe those who don't like pulp in their orange juice.

SERVES 4

THE STEW:

1½ lb (600 g) chuck roast or beef sirloin
2 carrots
¼ celery root (celeriac)
1 yellow onion
3 cloves garlic
1 stalk of lemongrass
½ red chili pepper
Butter and olive oil, for frying
⅓ cup (¾ dl) unsweetened grated coconut
¾ cup (2 dl) water
1¼ cup (3 dl) whipping cream
1 tsp salt
Freshly ground white or black pepper

ACCOMPANIMENT:

7 oz (200 g) egg noodles
1 bunch cilantro
1 lime

DIRECTIONS:

Start with the stew:

1. Cut the meat into thin strips. Peel the carrots and the celery root, and cut them into strips or dice them.

2. Peel and finely chop the onion and garlic.

3. Crush the lemongrass by pounding it with the back of a knife handle, or with a small hammer—yes, you read that correctly; it helps to release its flavor. Cut the chili pepper into strips and remove the seeds (don't forget to wash your hands afterward!).

4. Heat butter and oil in a large skillet and add the meat, carrots, celery root, onion, garlic, and coconut. Sauté for a bit over medium heat.

5. Add the water, whipping cream, crushed lemongrass, and strips of chili. Let the liquid cook down—a process called "reducing" in kitchen jargon—until there is only about half of the original liquid left. Season with salt and freshly ground pepper.

Time to cook the noodles:

6. Cook the noodles in a large saucepan with salted water. Follow the cooking instructions on the package.

Time to eat:

7. Strip the cilantro leaves from the stalks, and sprinkle the leaves over the stew. Cut the lime in half and squeeze the juice into the stew. Serve stew in a separate serving dish from the noodles.

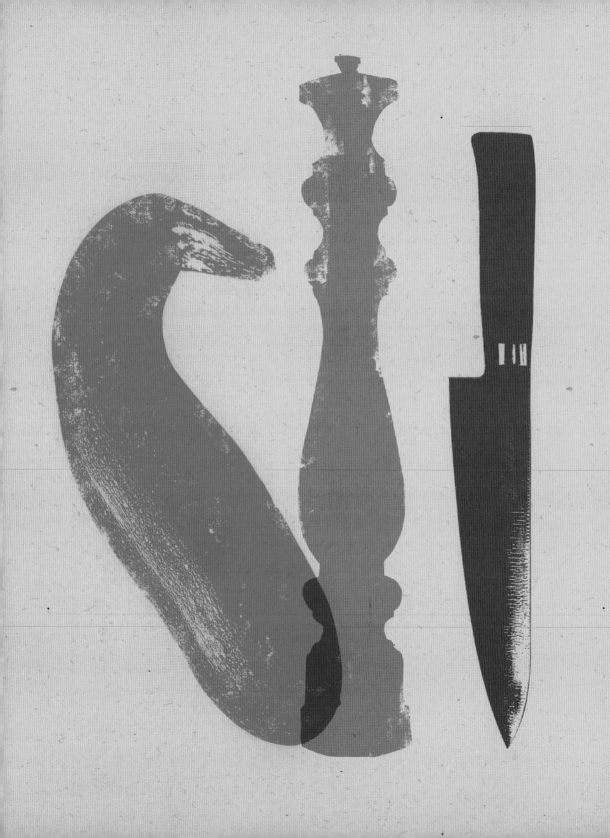

DAZZLE THE GROWNUPS

Some dishes are just meant to impress. I'm thinking of classics like oven-baked beef tenderloin with Bearnaise sauce or chicken soup Tom Kha Gai with that authentic Thai taste— not to mention the shredded meat in pulled pork, one of the easiest dishes you can make.

CHICKEN SOUP
Tom Kha Gai

Super simple to make, this soup still makes a great impression on anyone who has ever traveled to Thailand.

SERVES 4

1 yellow onion

2 garlic cloves

1 red chili pepper

1 stalk of lemongrass

¾-inch (2 cm) knob of fresh ginger

Oil, for frying

6 kaffir lime leaves

2 limes

2 cans (13½ fl oz or 400 ml/4 dl) of coconut milk

1¾ cups (4 dl) water

1½ tsp salt

3 tbsp fish sauce

2 skinless chicken breasts

ACCOMPANIMENT:

1 tbsp chopped cilantro

Chopped salted cashews or peanuts, optional

DIRECTIONS:

1. Peel and finely chop the onion and garlic. Halve, deseed, and cut the red chili pepper into strips (don't forget to wash your hands thoroughly afterward!). Crush the lemongrass by pounding it with a small hammer (yes, you read that right! It helps to release its flavor). Peel and finely chop the ginger; you should have about 2 tablespoons of it.

2. Pour the oil into a large saucepan and add in the onion, garlic, ginger, chili, lemongrass, and kaffir lime leaves. Sauté for about 2 minutes, or until the onion is soft but not browned.

3. Halve and press the limes. Add the lime juice, coconut milk, water, salt, and fish sauce to the saucepan, and let the soup simmer for about 15 minutes. Remove the soup from the heat, and let it rest for 5 minutes.

4. Cut the chicken breasts into strips. Bring the soup back to a boil again, and add in the chicken strips; let it all simmer for another 10 minutes. Lift out a piece of chicken and cut into it to see if it's ready; the meat shouldn't be pink. Note that the kaffir lime leaves are not to be eaten—they're only there to impart their flavor!

Time to eat:

5. Serve directly in soup bowls and sprinkle some chopped cilantro and maybe some cashews or peanuts over the warm soup.

ASIAN FLAVORS
Kaffir lime leaves and lemongrass are Asian ingredients that have great citrus flavor. You'll find them at well-stocked grocery stores.

HOW TO HANDLE RAW AND COOKED CHICKEN CORRECTLY
Wash the knife, the cutting board, and your hands thoroughly when you have handled and cut up raw chicken. It's also important to make sure that the chicken is cooked thoroughly before you eat it. The chicken is ready if its juices run clear, not pink, when you pierce the meat with a knife or a fork. If you use a meat thermometer, place it in the thickest part of the meat without touching bone—it should register 158°F (70°C).

FISH SAUCE
Real Thai fish sauce smells pretty strong, but it adds the right Asian salty flavor, so don't leave it out!

MOULES FRITES
(mussels with French fries)

It might seem strange to eat mussels with fries, but it is in fact a classic French dish.
To make the fries you'll need to use a deep fryer, so have an adult around to help you out.

SERVES 4

1 bag (2¼ lbs or 1 kg/1,000 g) of fresh mussels

2 shallots

3 garlic cloves

½ fennel bulb

Olive oil, for frying

¾ cup (2 dl) water

¾ cup (2 dl) whipping cream

1 tsp salt

½ cup (1 dl) parsley leaves

FRENCH FRIES:

4 baking potatoes

Oil for deep frying,
enough to fill your deep fryer

½ tsp salt

DIRECTIONS:

Begin with the mussels:

1. Rinse the mussels under running cold water, and scrub them with a hard brush. Remove their "beard," or the threads that anchored the mussel in the water. Tap on all the mussels, and throw away any that won't close.

2. Peel and finely chop the shallots and garlic. Cut the fennel bulb into strips about ⅛" thick.

3. Heat about 2 tablespoons of olive oil in a large, deep saucepan. Add in the onion, garlic, and fennel, and fry them over medium heat until they are soft but not browned. Add in the mussels, turn the heat up, and let them sweat on high for about 2 minutes.

4. Add in the water and the cream. Now, with the lid on the saucepan, let the mussels cook for about 5 minutes. Shake the saucepan a few times during this time. Season with salt.

5. Chop the parsley.

French fries:

6. Peel the potatoes and cut them into big strips ⅘ inch (2 cm) thick. Rinse them under cold water.

7. Boil the potatoes in salted water for 4 minutes. Drain the water and let the potatoes steam in the saucepan without the lid on. Dry the potatoes carefully with paper towels.

8. Heat the oil in the deep fryer to 356°F (180°C). Deep fry the potato strips in batches until they are golden brown; remove them with a skimmer and let them drain on a paper towel.

9. Season with salt and put the fries in a serving bowl.

Time to eat:

10. Place the mussels on a serving dish or in a big bowl and sprinkle with the parsley. Serve immediately with fries on the side, and preferably some good bread to mop up all the lovely sauce.

CHECK THOSE MUSSELS!

Only cook mussels that are closed (which means they are live mussels). If you find a mussel that's already open, tap it against the kitchen counter. If it closes then it's okay to cook; if not, throw it away. Throw away any mussels that didn't open while cooking.

THE BEST OIL FOR DEEP FRYING

Canola oil or sunflower oil are good for deep frying as they are neutral in taste. You can use the same oil several times over if you strain it thoroughly after using it.

OVEN-FRIED FRENCH FRIES

If you don't have access to a deep fryer, cook your fries in the oven instead. Place the parboiled potato strips on a baking sheet, drizzle oil over them, sprinkle with some salt, and roast them in the oven at 435°F (225°C) for 20 minutes.

SOLE GRATIN IN LOBSTER SAUCE
with broccoli and zucchini

This is a gratin I'm happy to make often. There is a very decadent feel to this dish,
even though it's so easy to make.

SERVES 4

8 fillets of sole or other flat fish

1 zucchini

1 small bunch of broccoli

2 garlic cloves

Olive oil, for frying

Salt

Freshly ground white or black pepper

1 can Campbell's Seafood Bisque soup

½ soup-can of whole milk, water, or
whipping cream

¾ cup (2 dl) whipping cream

1 large egg yolk

DIRECTIONS:

1. Preheat the oven to 480°F (250°C).

2. Season the fish with salt and freshly
ground pepper. Roll up the fillets, the
rougher side where the skin was attached
on the outside. Place the rolls in an
ovenproof baking dish.

3. Thinly slice the zucchini and broccoli,
along with the stems (they're edible, too!).
Break the broccoli florets apart. Peel and
finely chop the garlic.

4. Sauté the zucchini, broccoli, and
garlic in a skillet with some olive oil for a
few minutes. Season with salt and freshly
ground pepper. Place the vegetables in the
baking dish with the fish.

5. Mix the soup with half a can of milk,
water, or cream, and pour it over the
vegetables and the fish. Place the dish in
the oven and let it bake for 10 minutes.

6. While the fish is baking, whip the
whipping cream in a bowl and stir in the
egg yolk. Remove the dish from the oven
and place dollops of whipping cream over
the fish. Return the dish to the oven and
bake for another 5 minutes.

Time to eat:

7. Enjoy this fish gratin with riced
potatoes (see below) or rice (see p. 19).

RICED POTATOES ARE SCRUMPTIOUS!

Place a few cooked potatoes at a time in
a potato ricer and press down, or mash

by hand. You can do this with all types of
potatoes.

GRATIN? WHAT'S THAT?

It just means something is oven-baked
at high heat. A gratin's surface should be
nice and golden brown.

Learn how to crack open an egg on p. 17.

ROAST BEEF TENDERLOIN
with baked tomatoes, Béarnaise sauce, and small Hasselback potatoes

Beef tenderloin and stressed out cooks don't make a good team,
so handle the meat properly and don't try to rush this recipe.

SERVES 4

BEEF TENDERLOIN AND TOMATOES:

20 small cherry tomatoes on the vine

1 garlic clove

½ tbsp brown sugar

Salt

Freshly ground white or black pepper

Butter and olive oil, for frying

1¾ lbs (800 g) beef tenderloin

BÉARNAISE SAUCE:

7 oz (200 g) butter

1 shallot

1–2 tbsp butter, for frying

2 tsp dried French tarragon

4 tbsp white wine vinegar

¼ cup (½ dl) water

3 large egg yolks

1 bunch (⅔ oz or 20 g) fresh tarragon, chopped

Salt and freshly ground white or black pepper

HASSELBACK POTATOES:

1 bag (1¾ lb or 800 g) small fingerling potatoes

4 tbsp olive oil

2 tbsp bread crumbs

Sea salt and freshly ground black pepper

DIRECTIONS:

Start with the Hasselback potatoes:

1. Preheat the oven to 390°F (200°C).

2. Slice the potatoes thinly with a sharp knife, but don't cut them completely straight through, because the slices should remain attached at the bottom. (Put the potato in a wooden spoon; this will prevent the cuts from going all the way through).

3. Mix the olive oil, bread crumbs, salt, and freshly ground pepper in a bowl. Add in the potatoes and stir thoroughly. Place the potatoes in a dish, cut side up. Roast them on the middle rack of the oven for 35 to 40 minutes, or until they're golden brown and crisp.

Bake the tomatoes:

4. Increase the oven's temperature to 435°F (225°C).

5. Place the tomatoes and the garlic clove (crushed, peel and all) in an ovenproof dish and sprinkle with brown sugar. Season with salt and freshly ground pepper. Place the dish on the middle rack of the oven and bake the tomatoes for 10 to 15 minutes. Remove the dish, set it to the side, and decrease the oven's temperature to 230°F (110°C).

Cook the tenderloin:

6. Melt the butter and olive oil in a skillet. Place the tenderloin in the skillet and sear it on all sides for 3 to 5 minutes. Season with salt and freshly ground pepper. Place the tenderloin on an oven rack with a baking sheet underneath to catch the running meat juices. Insert a meat thermometer into the tenderloin and let the meat bake until the inner temperature registers 129.2°F (54°C) for a nice, pink meat. Remove the meat from the oven and let it rest, covered with a sheet of parchment paper, for about 10 minutes.

Make the Béarnaise sauce while the meat is in the oven:

7. Melt the butter in a small saucepan over medium heat.

8. Peel and finely chop the shallot. Melt a piece of butter in a skillet and fry the shallot and dried tarragon over medium heat. Add the vinegar and water, and let them cook down or reduce until you have about 2 tablespoons of liquid left.

9. Remove the saucepan from the heat and whisk in the egg yolks. Whisk for 1 minute. Then add the melted butter in a thin stream while you're whisking. Add the fresh tarragon leaves. Season with salt and freshly ground pepper.

Time to eat:

10. Cut the meat into nice slices. Serve with the baked tomatoes, Béarnaise sauce, and the Hasselback potatoes.

Learn how to crack open an egg on p. 17.

BAKED STUFFED PORK TENDERLOIN

with wheat berry salad, apples, and olives

Here's a taste of Italy! It's a feast for the eye, too, as we roll the tenderloin up with ham and basil.

SERVES 4

PORK TENDERLOIN WITH PROSCIUTTO AND BASIL:

1 pork tenderloin approx. 1¼ lb (600 g)

1–2 tbsp Dijon mustard

Salt

Freshly ground black pepper

8–10 slices prosciutto or air-cured ham

1 bunch fresh basil

WHEAT BERRY SALAD WITH APPLE AND OLIVES:

1¾ cup (4 dl) wheat berries

1 head Boston lettuce

½ red onion

¼ cup (½ dl) black olives, pitted

1 green apple

1 lemon

Olive oil, for drizzling

YOGURT SAUCE:

1¾ cup (4 dl) Turkish or Greek yogurt

1 tsp honey

Freshly ground black pepper

DIRECTIONS:

Start with the pork tenderloin:

1. Preheat the oven to 305°F (150°C).

2. Trim the sinew and fat from the tenderloin. Using a pastry brush, coat the tenderloin with some Dijon mustard. Season with salt and freshly ground black pepper.

3. Place a piece of plastic wrap on the kitchen counter. Lay down the slices of ham, overlapping them a bit, until they cover the plastic wrap. Chop the basil leaves and sprinkle them over the slices of ham. Place the tenderloin at the bottom edge of the plastic wrap. Lift the plastic wrap to move the tenderloin and the ham, and roll everything into a tight cylinder (removing the wrap as you roll!). When you're done, discard the plastic wrap. Wrap some kitchen twine around the meat roll to hold it together. Now the meat is ready to go into the oven.

4. Heat a little olive oil in a skillet and add the meat; sear it on all four sides. Insert a meat thermometer into the tenderloin so the tip is in the middle of the roll. If it's ovenproof, place the skillet in the oven; if not, transfer the meat to an ovenproof dish and put it in the oven. Roast the meat until the thermometer registers an internal temperature of 140°F–143.2°F (60°C–62°C).

5. Remove the meat from the oven and let it rest for about 5 minutes before slicing.

Make the salad and yogurt sauce while the tenderloin is in the oven:

6. Cook the wheat berries; check the package for cooking instructions.

7. Rinse the head of lettuce and cut it in half. Dry the pieces with paper towels. Peel and chop the red onion. Chop the olives. Wash the apple, dry, and grate it on the grater's coarse side.

8. Place the lettuce and the cooked wheat berries on a serving platter (where you've also left room for the meat). Sprinkle with red onion and olives. Cut the lemon in half, squeeze it in a citrus press or by hand, and pour the juice over the salad. Place the coarsely grated apple on top of the salad.

9. Pour the yogurt into a separate bowl. Drizzle with honey and sprinkle with coarsely ground black pepper.

Time to eat:

10. Cut the meat into decent-sized slices. Place the meat on a serving platter with the salad, and drizzle everything with some good olive oil. Serve with the yogurt, dig in, and enjoy!

PULLED PORK
with Chinese pancakes and "hojjsan" sauce

Simplicity itself! Put the pot in the oven on Saturday morning, and the meat will be ready by late afternoon. The hojjsan sauce is my own personal take on the Asian hoisin sauce.

SERVES 4–6

PULLED PORK:

3¼ lb (1 ½ kg or 1,500 g) boneless pork roast

¾ cup (2 dl) barbeque sauce

2 tbsp white wine vinegar

1 tbsp paprika

⅖ tsp (2 krm) cayenne pepper

Salt and freshly ground black pepper

HOJJSAN SAUCE:

1½ tbsp Kikkoman soy sauce

½ cup (1 dl) tahini (sesame seed paste)

2 tsp sesame oil

1 tsp sambal oelek

1 tsp instant coffee powder

2 tbsp white wine vinegar

3½ tbsp honey

CHINESE PANCAKES:

1¾ cup (4 dl) all-purpose flour

2 cups (5 dl) whole milk

4 large eggs

1 tsp salt

1 lemon

2 garlic cloves

Butter, for frying

ACCOMPANIMENT:

Lettuce leaves

Fresh cilantro leaves

DIRECTIONS:

Start with the meat:

1. Preheat the oven to 250°F (120°C).

2. Place the meat in an ovenproof Dutch oven with a lid. Mix the barbeque sauce, white wine vinegar, paprika, and cayenne pepper in a bowl and pour it over the meat. Place the Dutch oven, covered, in the oven and let it cook for 8 to 9 hours.

3. Remove the meat from the oven and pull it apart with a fork so it separates into strands. Season the meat with salt and freshly ground pepper.

Make the Hojjan sauce:

4. Combine all ingredients for the sauce in a bowl.

Make the pancakes:

5. Whisk the flour and milk together in a bowl. Add in the eggs, one at a time, and whisk thoroughly between each egg until you have a smooth batter. Season with salt.

6. Wash and finely grate the peel of a whole lemon. Squeeze the juice from half the lemon. Peel and finely grate the cloves of garlic. Add it all to the batter and mix well.

7. Place a pat of butter in a skillet and fry the pancakes one at a time over low heat. Use ⅓ cup (¾ dl) batter for each pancake and keep tipping the pan to make the batter spread evenly. Flip the pancake after

a bit; it will look slightly thinner and paler than regular pancakes.

Time to eat:

8. If the meat has cooled down, heat it up in the microwave. Set one pancake on each plate. Place a few lettuce leaves on top, and then pile on some pulled pork. Using a spoon, drizzle some hojjan sauce on top. Top with fresh cilantro, fold it like a wrap, and dig in!

TAHINI: WHAT'S THAT?

Tahini is a paste made from mashed sesame seeds. You'll find it in most grocery stores.

HOW TO GRATE, PEEL, AND JUICE A LEMON

Always wash lemons thoroughly with lukewarm water before you grate the peel. If you are going to use both the peel and the juice, finely grate the lemon peel first, then cut the lemon in half and squeeze out the juice.

HANGING OUT WITH FRIENDS

Invite your friends over and make some food together. Don't worry if it gets a bit messy in the kitchen; just have a great time rolling out pizza dough or cooking hamburgers. But . . . don't forget to clean up afterwards!

VEGETABLES AND CHIPS
with an assortment of dips

It's always a welcome sight—at least for me—to see a large platter of vegetables and chips with which to scoop up three different dips. All of them are equally yummy, so make them all.

SERVES 4–6

VEGETABLES:

1 hothouse (English) cucumber

3 carrots

½ head cauliflower

1 bunch broccoli

2 avocados

1 carton cherry tomatoes on the vine

1 bag romaine lettuce

1 bag (7 oz or 200 g) potato chips

SOUR CREAM AND ONION DIP:

½ lemon

1 garlic clove

1¼ cup (3 dl) sour cream

2 tsp onion powder

2 tbsp snipped chives

Salt

Freshly ground black pepper

SPICY THAI DIP:

1 garlic clove

1 green chili pepper

1 lime

¾ cup (2 dl) Turkish or Greek yogurt

½ cup (1 dl) sour cream

1 tbsp preserved chopped ginger, jarred

1 tbsp preserved chopped coriander, jarred or fresh

2 tsp sambal oelek

Salt

Freshly ground black pepper

HERB AND CHEESE DIP:

1¾ oz (50 g) aged hard cheese

1¾ oz (50 g) feta cheese

1¼ cups (3 dl) sour cream

¾ cup (2 dl) freshly chopped herbs (parsley, chives, basil, or dill)

Salt

Freshly ground black pepper

Olive oil

DIRECTIONS:

Cut up the vegetables:

1. Rinse all the vegetables except for the avocado. Peel the cucumber and the carrots and cut them into sticks. Separate the cauliflower and broccoli into small florets. Peel the avocado and remove the pit, and then cut the avocado into chunks.

Prepare the Sour Cream and Onion dip:

2. Squeeze the lemon. Peel and finely chop the garlic clove. Mix the lemon juice, garlic, and remaining ingredients, and season with salt and freshly ground pepper.

Prepare the Spicy Thai dip:

3. Peel and finely chop the garlic clove. Cut the chili pepper in half, remove all the seeds, and finely chop (don't forget to wash your hands thoroughly afterward!). Wash the lime and grate the peel on the grater's fine side. Cut the lime in half and squeeze out the juice. Mix the garlic, chili pepper, lime peel, and juice with the remaining ingredients, and season with salt and freshly ground pepper.

Prepare the Herb and Cheese dip:

4. Grate the cheese on the grater's fine side. Crumble the feta cheese or grate it on the grater's coarse side. Mix the hard cheese and feta with the remaining ingredients, and season with salt and freshly ground pepper. Drizzle with some olive oil.

Time to eat:

5. Arrange the vegetables and potato chips in bowls and use them to scoop the dips.

ITALIAN MEATBALLS
with tomato sauce

This could lead to a kiss, like in Walt Disney's *Lady and the Tramp.*

SERVES 4

MEATBALLS:

1 large egg

⅔ cup (1½ dl) whole milk

1 slice white bread

1 lemon

½ yellow onion

1 garlic clove

1¼ lb (500 g) ground veal or beef

½ cup (1 dl) freshly grated Parmesan

2 tsp dried French tarragon

1 tsp salt

Freshly ground white or black pepper

Butter and oil, for frying

TOMATO SAUCE:

1 shallot

3 garlic cloves

⅓ cup (¾ dl) cold-pressed olive oil

1 container cherry tomatoes on the vine

½ cup (1 dl) water

1 (14 oz or 400 g) can crushed tomatoes

1 tbsp white wine vinegar

½ tsp salt

Freshly ground white or black pepper

½ tsp granular sugar

ACCOMPANIMENT:

¼ cup (½ dl) pine nuts

Bucatini pasta

Basil leaves

DIRECTIONS:

Start with the meatballs:

1. Break the egg into a bowl, add in the milk, and whisk them together. Cut the crust off the bread, and add the bread to the egg/milk mixture to let the bread soak up the liquid and become soft. This should take about 10 minutes.

2. Meanwhile, wash and grate the lemon peel. Peel and finely chop the onion. Peel and grate the garlic on the grater's fine side.

3. Place the ground meat in the bowl and mix it with the soaked bread, lemon peel, onion, garlic, Parmesan, tarragon, salt, and freshly ground pepper. Let the meat mixture sit for 10 minutes.

4. Wet your hands and make the ground meat into meatballs. Heat butter and oil in a skillet and fry the meatballs in batches for about 10 minutes.

Prepare the tomato sauce:

5. Peel the shallot and garlic. Finely chop the shallot and crush the garlic.

6. Heat the olive oil in a saucepan and add the onion, garlic, and fresh tomatoes. Let everything cook until it simmers. Add the water and the crushed tomatoes, and let simmer again for 10 to 15 minutes. Season with vinegar, salt, freshly ground pepper, and a little sugar.

7. Add the fried meatballs to the sauce and let them simmer slowly for 10 minutes.

The accompaniments:

8. Toast the pine nuts in a dry skillet over medium heat. Keep a close eye on them, as they burn easily!

9. Cook the pasta in salt water in a large saucepan. Check the package for cooking instructions. Drain the water.

Time to eat:

10. Enjoy the meatballs with the sauce and freshly cooked pasta. Sprinkle with some toasted pine nuts and, if you like, garnish with fresh basil leaves.

GREAT LOOKING MEATBALLS

It's easier to make nice round meatballs when your hands are wet. Rinse your hands with cold water as you're working so the meat mixture doesn't stick to them.

A PINCH OF SUGAR FOR THE SAUCE

Real chefs always add a pinch of sugar to their tomato sauce. The sugar enhances the taste of the tomato while reducing the sauce's overall acidity.

HAMBURGERS

13-year-old Ebba gave me her recipe for these hamburgers with homemade buns and dressing. I couldn't have made them better myself!

SERVES 4

HAMBURGER BUNS:

¾ cup (2 dl) whole milk

1 tbsp corn syrup

1½ tbsp olive oil

4 tsp dried yeast

2 cups (5 dl) bread flour

1 tsp salt

1–2 tbsp sesame seeds

1 large egg, for glazing

HAMBURGER DRESSING:

3 ⅓ fl oz mayonnaise

1 tbsp Heinz chili sauce

1 tbsp gherkin relish

½ tbsp paprika

Freshly ground black pepper

HAMBURGERS:

1¼ lb (500 g) ground beef

1 large egg

1 tsp salt

Freshly ground black pepper

1 tsp paprika

Butter, for frying

ACCOMPANIMENT:

Shredded iceberg lettuce, tomato slices, hothouse (English) cucumber slices, cheese slices, red onion rings

DIRECTIONS:

Start with the buns:

1. Preheat the oven to 390°F (200°C).

2. Pour milk, syrup, and olive oil into a saucepan and heat it until it is lukewarm.

3. Put the yeast in a bowl, pour the baking liquid over it, and stir until the yeast has dissolved. Mix in the flour and then the salt. Mix with a wooden spoon at the beginning, and then knead the dough with your hands until it's no longer sticky and comes away from the sides of the bowl. Set a kitchen towel over the dough and let it rise for 30 minutes.

4. Dust the kitchen counter with some flour and turn out the dough onto it. Divide the dough into four equal sections, and form each section into a nice and smooth bun. Transfer the buns to a baking sheet lined with parchment paper.

5. Brush the buns lightly with some water and sprinkle the tops of them with sesame seeds. Let the buns rise on the baking sheet for 25 minutes.

6. Break the egg into a bowl and whisk it with a fork. Brush the buns lightly with the egg wash. Place the baking sheet on the middle rack of the oven and bake the buns for 8 minutes. They should be deliciously golden brown. Place the freshly baked buns on a rack to cool.

Make the dressing:

7. Mix all the ingredients for the dressing in a bowl. Season with freshly ground black pepper.

Cook the hamburgers:

8. Place the ground meat, egg, and spices in a bowl and mix together quickly. Wet your hands and grab a big dollop of the meat mixture. Shape it into a hamburger; do the same with the remaining meat mixture until you have four hamburgers.

9. Heat butter in a skillet or grill pan (the hamburgers will get nice grill marks if cooked on a grill pan) and fry the hamburgers for about 3 to 4 minutes on each side.

Time to eat:

10. Assemble the hamburgers with the buns, hamburger dressing, and sides to your liking. Enjoy!

WORK QUICKLY

Never take too long when stirring or mixing ground meat, because it makes the hamburgers or meatballs feel dry and taste bland.

CHICKEN NUGGETS
with yogurt cucumber dip

SERVES 4

CHICKEN NUGGETS:

1 ⅓ lb (600 g) boneless chicken thighs

Salt

Freshly ground black pepper

2 cups (5 dl) Panko breadcrumbs

Flaky sea salt

BATTER:

1¾ cup (4 dl) sparkling water

1¾ cup (4 dl) all-purpose flour

1 tsp salt

1 tbsp honey

3 tbsp baking powder

YOGURT CUCUMBER DIP:

½ hothouse cucumber (English)

1 garlic clove

¾ cup (2 dl) Turkish yogurt

2 tbsp crème fraîche

2 tbsp chopped lemon balm or mint

2 tbsp olive oil

½ tsp salt

ACCOMPANIMENT:

Leafy greens such as arugula, Swiss chard, or spinach; lemon wedges.

DIRECTIONS:

Start with the dip:

1. Peel the cucumber and grate it on the grater's coarse side. Place the grated cucumber in a sieve over a bowl or the sink, and sprinkle the cucumber with salt. Let it sit for 20 minutes, and then squeeze out the juice with your hands.

2. Peel and grate the garlic on the grater's fine side.

3. Mix together the yogurt, crème fraîche, and cucumber in a bowl. Stir in the grated garlic, lemon balm or mint, and olive oil. Season with salt.

Prepare the chicken:

4. Cut each chicken thigh into three pieces. Season each piece with salt and freshly ground pepper.

5. Mix all the ingredients for the batter. Pour the Panko crumbs onto a plate.

6. First, dip the chicken into the batter, and then dredge it in the Panko crumbs. Make sure that the pieces of chicken are covered in crumbs on all sides. Set the prepared pieces on a platter covered with paper towels.

7. In a deep fryer, heat the oil to 355°F (180°C). Cook the chicken in batches for 3 to 5 minutes; the pieces should be crispy and golden brown. Check that the chicken is fully cooked by cutting through a piece and making sure the meat is not pink. Place the fried chicken on a platter covered with paper towels to soak up some of the oil. Sprinkle with flaky sea salt.

Time to eat:

8. Dunk the chicken in the dip, and enjoy with a salad of mixed greens and a squeeze of lemon juice.

DEEP FRYING IN A SAUCEPAN
If you don't have a deep fryer but an adult is around to give you a hand, you can deep fry in a saucepan instead. You'll need to heat the oil to 355°F (180°C) and deep fry the chicken a few pieces at a time. If the oil catches fire, quickly place a lid over the pan to smother the flames. Never try to put out burning oil with water; it will only burn more fiercely. That being said, you will get best results if you use a real deep fryer.

PIZZA 3 FORMAGGIO
with tomato salad and chili dressing

Italian, once again! It's just so good with three different formaggio (Italian for cheese) on the pizza!

SERVES 4

PIZZA DOUGH:

4 tsp dried yeast

1 cup (2½ dl) lukewarm water

½ tsp salt

2½ cups (6 dl) bread flour

2 tbsp olive oil

TOPPINGS:

1 small red onion

¾ cup (2 dl) walnuts

2 bags (4½ oz or 125 g) mozzarella

7 oz (200 g) goat cheese

8 oz (225 g) full fat cheese

Olive oil

¼ cup (½ dl) honey

Flaky sea salt

TOMATO SALAD AND CHILI DRESSING:

2 containers (1½ lb or 600 g) cherry tomatoes

1 garlic clove

½ red chili pepper

Small bunch chives

1 tbsp balsamic vinegar

2 tbsp apple cider vinegar

3 tbsp olive oil

1 tsp sesame oil

1 tbsp honey

Salt

DIRECTIONS:

Start by making the pizza dough:

1. In a bowl, dissolve the yeast in some of the lukewarm water. Add the rest of the water, salt, and bread flour. Stir together with a wooden spoon, and then knead it a bit with your hands. Place a towel over the dough in the bowl, and let the dough rise for 45 minutes.

Make the salad and dressing:

2. Cut the tomatoes in half or in wedges, and place them on a platter. Peel and finely chop the garlic. Cut and deseed the chili pepper. Finely chop the chili and the chives (wash your hands thoroughly afterward!).

3. Mix the balsamic vinegar, apple cider vinegar, olive oil, sesame oil, and honey in a bowl. Stir in garlic, chili pepper, and chives. Season with salt.

Assemble the pizza:

4. For the toppings, peel the onion, cut it in half, and slice it into half-moon slices. Chop the walnuts. Break the mozzarella and goat cheese into coarse chunks. Grate the full-fat cheese on the grater's fine side.

5. Heat the oven to 465°F (240°C). Place a baking sheet in the oven to warm it up.

6. Transfer the pizza dough to a floured kitchen counter. Cut the dough in half and roll each piece out thinly with a rolling pin. Set the dough on a sheet of parchment

paper and drizzle with some olive oil. Cover with the mozzarella, goat cheese, and grated cheese, and then place the sliced onion on top of the cheese.

7. Remove the warm baking sheet from the oven, and carefully transfer the pizza and parchment paper onto the baking sheet (be careful not to burn yourself on the hot baking sheet!). Put the baking sheet back in the oven and bake the pizza for 10 to 15 minutes, or until it is golden brown and the cheese has melted.

8. Sprinkle the whole pizza with nuts and drizzle with some honey; top with some flaky sea salt.

Time to eat:

9. Cut the pizza into slices (you can do this really easily with kitchen shears). Drizzle the dressing over the tomato salad, dig in to the pizza, and enjoy the salad on the side.

SHAKE IT, BABY!

Pour all the ingredients for the dressing into a glass jar, screw on the lid, and shake. It's easier to mix the dressing that way to make it smooth and fine.

TACO PIE

When you're bored with tacos, make a taco pie. Easy-peasy!

SERVES 6

PIE CRUST:

1¾ oz (50 g) butter, softened

1¾ cup (4 dl) all-purpose flour

⅔ cup (1½ dl) whole milk

2 tsp baking powder

½ tsp salt

GROUND MEAT FILLING:

2 yellow onions or 2 large shallots

2 garlic cloves

Oil, for frying

1¾ lb (800 g) ground beef or half pork/half beef

1 tsp salt

Freshly ground white or black pepper

TACO SEASONING:

3 tsp dried coriander

3 tsp dried Mexican oregano

2 tsp paprika

3 tsp cumin

⅕ tsp (1 krm) cayenne pepper

TOPPING:

2 cups (5 dl) crème fraîche

4 tbsp mayonnaise

1¾ cup (4 dl) grated aged cheddar cheese

ACCOMPANIMENT:

1 bag (2½ oz or 70 g) mixed lettuce

DIRECTIONS:

Start with the pie crust:

1. Preheat the oven to 390°F (200°C).

2. With your hands, quickly knead all the ingredients into a dough. Dust the kitchen counter with flour, tip out the dough, and roll it out with a rolling pin. Place it in a pie pan, making sure it covers the bottom and the sides.

Make the ground meat filling:

3. Peel the onions or shallots and slice them thinly. Peel and crush the garlic.

4. Heat oil in a skillet and cook the onions/shallots and garlic until they are lightly browned. Push the onions/shallots toward the edge of the skillet, and then brown the ground meat along with the taco seasoning (coriander, Mexican oregano, paprika, cumin, and cayenne pepper).

5. Mix the onions/shallots back in once the ground meat has browned. Season with salt and freshly ground pepper. Fill the crust with the meat mixture.

6. Mix crème fraîche and mayonnaise in a separate bowl. Spread the mixture over the meat filling, and top with the grated cheese.

Bake the pie:

7. Place the pie pan on the middle rack of the oven, and bake for 20 to 30 minutes.

Time to eat:

8. Enjoy the pie warm, accompanied by a fresh green salad.

QUICKLY DOES IT

It's important to not overwork the dough if you want a crisp and delicious piecrust.

MAKE YOUR OWN TACO SEASONING

Make a large batch of taco seasoning, and save the leftovers in a glass jar with a lid. You can also use it to season meatballs.

SWEETS

I believe I'm in good company in craving something sweet at the end of dinner. Next up you have some truly decadent desserts to choose from: Nutella mousse, Rocky Road ice cream cake, and Raspberry Mazarin with Turkish pepper candy. Why choose just one when you can make them all!

NUTELLA MOUSSE
with crunchy Krispies and fresh raspberries

This luscious dessert both melts and crunches in your mouth.
Everyone will want seconds, and even thirds!

SERVES 4

NUTELLA MOUSSE:
1¼ cup (3 dl) whipping cream
½ cup (1 dl) Nutella

CRUNCHY TOPPING:
1 tbsp confectioner's sugar
½ cup (1 dl) Rice Krispies

ACCOMPANIMENT:
1 container fresh raspberries,
4½ oz (125 g)

DIRECTIONS:

Start with the Nutella mousse:

1. Pour ¼ cup (½ dl) of the whipping cream into a bowl. Add Nutella in dollops and stir until you have a smooth cream.

2. Whip the rest of the heavy cream until quite firm (but be careful not to whip it too long, or you could easily end up with butter instead!). Fold the cream into the Nutella mixture to make a mousse. Place the mousse in the refrigerator and let it set for about an hour.

Make the crunchy Krispies :

3. Heat a skillet and add the sugar and the Rice Krispies and stir. The sugar must become very hot and melt into a brown liquid, which is a caramel (DO NOT put your finger in it to taste it; you'll burn yourself!). The Rice Krispies should turn golden brown on the surface. Place the crunchy Krispies on a piece of parchment paper to cool down (be careful, as it is very hot!).

Time to eat:

4. Layer the mousse and the raspberries in four decorative glasses. Top the mousse with plenty of crunchy Krispies. Yum!

CRUNCHY ICE CREAM TOPPING
If you have any leftover crunchy Krispies, save them in a glass jar to later sprinkle over ice cream.

CRÈME BRÛLÉE
with warm blueberries

This is a restaurant-caliber dessert, so it's not all that simple to make. However, if it doesn't come out great on your first try, practice makes perfect!

SERVES 4

CRÈME BRÛLÉE:

1 vanilla bean

1¾ cup (4 dl) whipping cream

½ cup (1 dl) whole milk

5 large egg yolks

½ cup (1 dl) granular sugar

2 tbsp raw cane sugar

WARM BLUEBERRIES:

8¾ oz (250 g) blueberries

1 tbsp granular sugar

DIRECTIONS:

Start with the crème brûlée:

1. Preheat the oven to 230°F (110°C).

2. Slice the vanilla bean in half lengthwise and scrape the seeds into a saucepan. Pour in the cream and milk, and add in the empty vanilla pod. Let it all come to a boil. Remove the saucepan from the heat and set it aside.

3. Stir (don't whisk!) the egg yolks and sugar. Pour the egg mixture into the cream/vanilla mixture in the saucepan and stir carefully until all the sugar is melted. Remove the vanilla pod.

4. Pour the egg/cream/vanilla mixture into four ovenproof ramekins. Fill a rectangular baking pan with some water and place the ramekins in it (the water should come about halfway up the sides of the ramekins) and place the pan in the oven. Bake for about 45 to 60 minutes, until the crème brûlées have set on the surface. Remove the ramekins from the oven and let them cool a little, then set them in the refrigerator to chill completely.

5. Turn on the oven to 480°F (250°C). Sprinkle the raw cane sugar over the crème brûlées. Place the ramekins on a baking sheet on the highest rack in the oven so the sugar can melt and brown.

Prepare the warm blueberries:

6. Heat the blueberries in a saucepan and carefully stir in the sugar.

Time to eat:

7. Eat the crème brûlée straight out of the ramekins, and serve the blueberries in a separate bowl.

FLAVOR THE CRÈME BRÛLÉE

Why not infuse a different flavor to the crème brûlée by adding 1 tablespoon of cocoa or ⅕ teaspoon (1 krm) ground cardamom instead of using vanilla? Adding ½ tablespoon of finely grated lemon or orange peel is also lovely.

Learn how to crack open an egg on p. 17.

ROCKY ROAD ICE CREAM CAKE

You can't possibly go wrong with these mouthwatering ingredients.
To bake this cake, you'll need a round, springform pan that's 9½" (24 cm) in diameter.

SERVES 8–10

1 pre-baked layer of meringue
7 oz (200 g) dark or milk chocolate
2 quarts (2 liters/20 dl) vanilla ice cream
½ cup (1 dl) coarsely chopped hazelnuts
½ cup (1 dl) salted peanuts
¾ cup (2 dl) mini marshmallows
1 jar (7 oz or 200 g) marshmallow fluff

DIRECTIONS:

1. Line the bottom of a springform baking pan with plastic wrap, or wedge a sheet of parchment paper between the bottom of the pan and its sides. Place the layer of meringue in the bottom of the pan.

2. Chop the chocolate coarsely with a knife.

3. Mix the ice cream with the chocolate, hazelnuts, peanuts, and marshmallows. Put the ice cream on top of the layer of meringue, and pat it down. Place this gorgeous treat in the freezer and let chill for 15 minutes.

4. Remove the pan from the freezer and spread the marshmallow fluff over the ice cream. Place the pan back in the freezer.

Time to eat:

5. Turn the oven temperature to 480°F (250°C). Remove the pan from the freezer, place it on the oven's highest rack, and leave the oven door open while the fluff turns golden brown; this will only take a few minutes! Remove the pan from the oven and loosen the cake around the edges. Serve immediately!

LEFTOVER ICE CREAM?

If you have any leftover ice cream cake, simply return the pan to the freezer. Don't forget to wrap it in plastic wrap so it stays delicious for the next helping.

BAKED APPLES
with cinnamon and digestive biscuit filling

Instead of making a regular apple pie, I decided to stuff the crumb filling inside the apples.
If you prefer, you can use Marie biscuits or other sweet-meal biscuits instead of digestive biscuits.

SERVES 4

BAKED APPLES WITH CINNAMON AND DIGESTIVE BISCUIT FILLING:

8 small apples

8 digestive biscuits

½ cup (1 dl) hazelnuts

5¼ oz (150 g) butter, softened

3 tbsp granular sugar

1 tbsp ground cinnamon

8 cinnamon sticks

Light corn syrup

VANILLA CUSTARD:

½ vanilla bean

1¾ cups (4 dl) whole milk

3 large egg yolks

1½ tbsp granular sugar

2 tsp cornstarch (Maizena)

¾ cup (2 dl) whipping cream

DIRECTIONS:

Start with the vanilla custard:

1. Slice the vanilla bean in half lengthwise and scrape the seeds into a saucepan. Pour in the milk, and add in the empty vanilla pod. Bring the mixture to a boil, then lower the heat to medium and let it simmer for 3 to 4 minutes, whisking all the while. Remove the saucepan from the heat and set it aside for 10 minutes.

2. Whisk the egg yolks with sugar and cornstarch in a separate bowl. Stir in the warm vanilla milk. Pour it all back into the saucepan and let it gently simmer until it thickens. Stir with a whisk. Remove the vanilla pod.

3. Place the saucepan in the sink and fill the sink with cold water. Stir the sauce until it cools. Place the sauce in the refrigerator until it has chilled completely.

4. Whip the cream and fold it into the cold vanilla sauce (custard).

Prepare the stuffed apples:

5. Preheat the oven to 355°F (180°C).

6. Remove the apple cores. Cut off the top of each apple to make lids. Set the apples in an ovenproof dish.

7. Crumble the digestive biscuits into a bowl. Chop the hazelnuts finely. Mix the hazelnuts, butter, sugar, and cinnamon in the bowl with the biscuit crumbs. Stir so everything is well combined. Stuff the mixture into the holes of the apples and set their lids on top.

8. Push a cinnamon stick through the lid of each apple and drizzle with syrup.

9. Put the dish in the oven and bake the apples for about 20 to 30 minutes, or until they are soft.

Time to eat:

10. Enjoy these lovely apples warm with some vanilla custard.

PREPARE THE DESSERT

You can prepare everything up to step 7 the day before. Place the dish in the refrigerator. You can finish up steps 8, 9, and 10 the next day.

Learn how to crack open an egg on p. 17.

PEAR AND RASPBERRY MAZARIN

with soft-serve ice cream and Turkish pepper candy

This is a classic Swedish sheet cake and an absolutely wonderful dessert that you simply won't be able to get enough of. If you don't like licorice, skip the Turkish pepper on the ice cream.

SERVES 8–10

PEAR AND RASPBERRY MAZARIN:

5¼ oz (150 g) almond paste

½ lemon

4½ oz (125 g) butter, softened

4½ oz (125 g) granular sugar

3 large eggs

⅓ cup (¾ dl) all-purpose flour

2 pears, peeled

4½ oz (125 g) frozen raspberries

2 tbsp pearl sugar

SOFT-SERVE ICE CREAM:

2¼ cups (5 dl) vanilla ice cream

¾ cup (2 dl) Russian yogurt

2 ⅔ oz (75 g) Turkish pepper candy

DIRECTIONS:

Make the Mazarin cake:

1. Preheat the oven to 350°F (175°C). Grate the almond paste on the grater's fine side. Wash the lemon and finely grate the peel. Cut the lemon in half and squeeze out its juice.

2. Place the grated almond paste in a bowl. With an electric mixer, whip it with the soft butter, sugar, lemon peel, and juice until fluffy.

3. Break the eggs into the mixture, one at a time. Stir thoroughly between the addition of each egg, and then stir in the flour.

4. Cut the pears into big wedges (and remove the cores).

5. Pour the batter into a greased baking pan. Add in the pear wedges in a nice pattern, and sprinkle with the raspberries and pearl sugar.

6. Place the pan on the middle rack of the oven and bake for 30 minutes, or until the cake is golden brown and has set.

Whip together the ice cream:

7. Let the ice cream soften a little bit. Whip it (this will be easiest if done with an electric mixer) with the yogurt until it looks like a smooth, soft-serve ice cream. Work as quickly as you can so the ice cream doesn't have time to melt.

Time to eat:

8. Crush the Turkish pepper candy with a mortar and pestle or hit the bag with a rolling pin. Sprinkle the crushed candy over the ice cream and eat with the Mazarin cake. Mmmmm!

WHAT ON EARTH HAPPENED TO THE BATTER?

Don't panic when you add the eggs and the batter looks like it's cracking. Simply add a tiny amount of flour and stir, and the batter should become smooth again. Everything is A-OK!

CONVERSION CHARTS

METRIC AND IMPERIAL CONVERSIONS

(These conversions are rounded for convenience)

Ingredient	Cups/Tablespoons/ Teaspoons	Ounces	Grams/Milliliters
Butter	1 cup = 16 tablespoons = 2 sticks	8 ounces	230 grams
Cheese, shredded	1 cup	4 ounces	110 grams
Cream cheese	1 tablespoon	0.5 ounce	14.5 grams
Cornstarch	1 tablespoon	0.3 ounce	8 grams
Flour, all-purpose	1 cup/1 tablespoon	4.5 ounces/0.3 ounce	125 grams/8 grams
Flour, whole wheat	1 cup	4 ounces	120 grams
Fruit, dried	1 cup	4 ounces	120 grams
Fruits or veggies, chopped	1 cup	5 to 7 ounces	145 to 200 grams
Fruits or veggies, puréed	1 cup	8.5 ounces	245 grams
Honey, maple syrup, or corn syrup	1 tablespoon	.75 ounce	20 grams
Liquids: cream, milk, water, or juice	1 cup	8 fluid ounces	240 milliliters
Oats	1 cup	5.5 ounces	150 grams
Salt	1 teaspoon	0.2 ounce	6 grams
Spices: cinnamon, cloves, ginger, or nutmeg (ground)	1 teaspoon	0.2 ounce	5 milliliters
Sugar, brown, firmly packed	1 cup	7 ounces	200 grams
Sugar, white	1 cup/1 tablespoon	7 ounces/0.5 ounce	200 grams/12.5 grams
Vanilla extract	1 teaspoon	0.2 ounce	4 grams

OVEN TEMPERATURES

Fahrenheit	Celsius	Gas Mark
225°	110°	$1/4$
250°	120°	$1/2$
275°	140°	1
300°	150°	2
325°	160°	3
350°	180°	4
375°	190°	5
400°	200°	6
425°	220°	7
450°	230°	8

Index

A

Apples, baked with cinnamon and digestive biscuit filling *90*

Asian beef stew with noodles *46*

B

Baked apples with cinnamon and digestive biscuit filling *90*

Baked tomatoes *58*

Bearnaise sauce *58*

Beef stew, Asian with noodles *58*

Beet salad *38*

Bread

    Hamburger bun *73*

    Scones *27*

C

Cardamom scones with Parmesan cheese and Parma ham *27*

Cauliflower soup with chili and lime *37*

Chicken nuggets with yogurt and cucumber dip *74*

Chicken soup Tom Kha Gai *53*

Chinese pancakes *62*

Chocolate whipped cream *24*

Crème brûlée with warm blueberries *86*

Crunchy Krispies with Rice Krispies *85*

D

Dips *69*

F

French fries *54*

Fruit salad with pineapple, passion fruit, and mint *31*

G

Granola with nuts and chocolate *28*

H

Hamburger bun *73*

Hamburger dressing *73*

Hamburgers *73*

Herb and cheese dip *69*

Hojjsan sauce *62*

I

Ice cream cake, Rocky Road *89*

Ice cream, soft-serve *93*

Italian meatballs with tomato sauce *70*

M

Mazarin, pear and raspberry with soft-serve ice cream and Turkish pepper *93*

Meatballs, Italian, with tomato sauce *70*

Meatloaf with Parmesan mashed potatoes and green salad *42*

Meat sauce, see Ragu Bolognese

Moroccan rice *41*

Moules frites (mussels with fries) *54*

Mussels, see Moules Frites

Müesli, see Granola

N

Nutella mousse with crunchy Krispies and fresh raspberries *85*

O

Oven-baked stuffed pork tenderloin with wheat berry salad, apples, and olives *61*

P

Pancakes

    Chinese *62*

Peach Melba smoothie *23*

Pear and raspberry Mazarin cake with soft-serve ice cream and Turkish pepper *93*

Pie, taco *78*

Pizza 3 formaggio with tomato salad and chili dressing *77*

Potatoes

    French fries *54*

    Hasselback *58*

    Parmesan mashed potatoes *42*

Pulled pork and Chinese pancakes and 'Hojjsan' sauce *62*

R

Ragu Bolognese *45*

Roasted beef tenderloin with baked tomatoes, Bearnaise sauce and

small Hasselback potatoes *58*
Rocky Road ice cream cake *89*

S

Salad
  Beet *38*
  Tomato, with chili dressing 77
  Wheat berry, apples, and olives *61*
Salmon and pasta gratin with beet
  salad *38*
Sausage stroganoff with Moroccan
  rice *41*
Sauce
  Bearnaise sauce *58*
  Dip *69*
  Hamburger dressing *73*

Hojjsan *62*
Tomato *70*
  Yogurt and cucumber dip 74
Scones, cardamom, with Parmesan
  cheese and Parma ham *27*
Smoothie, Peach Melba *23*
Soft-serve ice cream with Turkish
  pepper candy *93*
Sole gratin in lobster sauce with
  broccoli and zucchini *57*
Soup
  Cauliflower, with chili and lime *37*
  Chicken soup Tom Kha Gai *53*
Sour cream and onion dip *69*
Spicy Thai dip *69*

T

Taco seasoning *78*
Taco pie *78*
Tom Kha Gai, see Chicken soup
Tomato salad with chili dressing *77*
Tomato sauce *70*

V

Vegetables and chips with various
  dips *69*

W

Wheat berry salad with apple and
  olives *61*

Y

Yogurt and cucumber dip *74*

Many thanks for your help with preparing the food!

ARVID ANDERSSON
LI JANSDOTTER
JOJJE HURTIG
AKSER LIDÉN
NOREA LYCKE

COPYRIGHT © 2015 TINA NORDSTRÖM
PHOTOGRAPHY: JENNY GRIMSGÅRD
FIRST PUBLISHED BY BONNIER FAKTA, STOCKHOLM, SWEDEN
TRANSLATION COPYRIGHT © 2017 BY SKYHORSE PUBLISHING

SKYHORSE PUBLISHING BOOKS MAY BE PURCHASED IN BULK AT SPECIAL DISCOUNTS FOR SALES PROMOTION, CORPORATE GIFTS, FUND-RAISING, OR EDUCATIONAL PURPOSES.SPECIAL EDITIONS CAN ALSO BE CREATED TO SPECIFICATIONS. FOR DETAILS, CONTACT THE SPECIAL SALES DEPARTMENT, SKYHORSE PUBLISHING, 307 WEST 36TH STREET, 11TH FLOOR, NEW YORK, NY 10018 OR INFO@SKYHORSEPUBLISHING.COM.

SKYHORSE® AND SKYHORSE PUBLISHING® ARE REGISTERED TRADEMARKS OF SKYHORSE PUBLISHING, INC.®, A DELAWARE CORPORATION.

VISIT OUR WEBSITE AT WWW.SKYHORSEPUBLISHING.COM.

10 9 8 7 6 5 4 3 2 1

LIBRARY OF CONGRESS CATALOGING-IN-PUBLICATION DATA IS AVAILABLE ON FILE.

COVER DESIGN: JANE SHEPPARD

RECIPE DEVELOPMENT: BENNY CEDERBERG

GRAPHICS AND ILLUSTRATIONS: LUKAS MÖLLERSTEN, LYTH & CO

STYLING AND TEST KITCHEN: VICTORIA NORDSTRÖM

REPRO: ITALGRAF MEDIA, STOCKHOLM

ISBN: 978-1-5107-1706-0

EBOOK ISBN: 978-1-5107-1711-4

PRINTED IN CHINA